3 1994 01018 7760

SANTA ANA PUBLIC LIBRARY
NEWHOPE BRANCH

D0618117

WORKING IN

MUSIC

exploring
careers

WORKING IN
Music

By Barbara Lee
Introduction by Barbara Sher

Lerner Publications Company • Minneapolis

J 780.23 LEE
Lee, Barbara
Working in music

$22.95
NEWHOPE   31994010187760

For Ben, Molly, and Timothy

Acknowledgments
My thanks to the dozen people profiled in
this book, who freely gave me hours of their
time. And thanks also to the many friends
and strangers—too many to name here—
who helped me find just the right people
to interview.

The Exploring Careers series
was developed by Barbara Lee.

Copyright © 1996 by Barbara Lee
All rights reserved. International copyright secured. No part of this
book may be reproduced or transmitted in any form or by any
means, electronic or mechanical, including photocopying and
recording, or by any information retrieval system, without
permission in writing from Lerner Publications Company, except for
the inclusion of brief quotations in an acknowledged review.

Library of Congress Cataloging-in-Publication Data

Lee, Barbara, 1945–
    Working in Music / by Barbara Lee ; introduction
  by Barbara Sher.
      p.   cm. — (Exploring careers)
    Includes index.
    Summary: Outlines the careers of twelve people who work in
  the world of music, including a composer, recording engineer, and
  jazz drummer.
    ISBN 0-8225-1761-2 (alk. paper)
    1. Music—Vocational guidance—Juvenile literature. [1. Music—
  Vocational guidance. 2. Vocational guidance.] I. Title. II. Series:
  Exploring careers (Minneapolis, Minn.)
  ML3928.L44 1996
  780'.23—dc20   95-4694

Manufactured in the United States of America
1 2 3 4 5 6 – JR – 01 00 99 98 97 96

CONTENTS

INTRODUCTION

by Barbara Sher

Welcome to the world of work. It's a remarkable world, filled with opportunities, almost too big to understand. There are indoor jobs and outdoor jobs. There are jobs that involve other people and jobs that don't. There are jobs you've never heard of and jobs with names you can't pronounce. And to complicate matters even more, the jobs of tomorrow may not be the same as the jobs of today.

But some things will remain the same. In fact, let me tell you a secret. For successful people, work is like play. That's right—play. That's because they've found the work that is best suited to who they are. Their careers fit their unique talents, their interests, and their skills and education.

Begin by asking yourself what you love doing. What is fun? What makes you excited? The answers will give you some clues about what kind of work you might enjoy—and be good at. It's not too early to begin exploring. Talk to your teachers and parents, your friends and neighbors. Ask them to introduce you to people doing work that you would

like to find out more about. You will be surprised by how willing people are to talk about what they do. Perhaps they will even show you around their workplaces.

Reading this book is a great start. Without leaving your chair, you will go to work with people who will tell you about what they do and why they do it. They will give you ideas. Maybe their jobs will seem boring or hard. Or maybe they'll excite you. It doesn't matter. It's all part of exploring.

So let yourself be curious. Be a detective. Remember, you don't have to make up your mind right now. You are just collecting information. Good luck. And have fun!

TWELVE CAREERS IN MUSIC

A tourist in New York climbs out of the subway, a map and concert ticket in his hand. He looks around for the concert hall, realizes he is lost, then stops a woman on the street.

"How do I get to Carnegie Hall?" the tourist asks.

"Practice, practice, practice," says the New Yorker. It's an old joke, but it's still true. If you want to perform in Carnegie Hall—or on MTV—you have to practice. A lot.

There are hundreds of ways to work with music. Only a few of them will get you to Carnegie Hall. But all of them allow you to work in the extraordinary world of music. And that is what this book is about—some of the many appealing careers open to people who are interested in music. Although some of these careers may be obvious, others are often overlooked.

In the following pages, 12 successful people—including several full-time performers—take you behind the scenes and into their musical worlds. Their stories shed light on what it takes to be a recording engineer or a classical pianist, a DJ or a composer. Most are trained musicians, but some are not. Some of the 12 found music early in life, some later. Some have had unexpected, zigzagging career paths. Others have pursued musical careers from an early age. Many have more than one job. Some are on the cutting edge of technology. Others do things the old-fashioned way. Each is different.

But if you think that an opera administrator has nothing in common with a jazz drummer, think again. Although these people have diverse backgrounds and musical interests, they have more in common than you might expect. Underlying the success of each person is hard work, individual talent, and a willingness to improve and keep learning. Most of all, each has chosen to work in the exciting world of music. Not one of these people lost hope when their work lives didn't go their way. Instead they believed in themselves, sometimes changed directions or learned new skills, and made their own opportunities.

All of these people will honestly tell you what they like and don't like about what they do. Each person will have practical tips and suggestions to help you explore a musical career.

Twelve people. Twelve musical careers. Their stories may surprise you.

Carol Nethen

Chapter One

COMPOSER

omposer Carol Nethen writes music in a sunny attic while her dog snoozes in the door way. She is surrounded by 11 synthesizers, 3 keyboards, a powerful personal computer, a mixing board that lets her change and control the music, a television screen, VCR, and stereo speakers. Her attic looks like a small recording studio.

"There's a lot happening at once," she says as she adjusts dials. For Carol the technology is a necessary tool. "The secret to my success is that I know the traditional ways of making music *and* the new ways," she says. "All musical experiences are important. Everything becomes your music. It's the most wonderful thing about being a composer."

The Life of a Freelance Composer

Carol is an independent film and television composer. As a composer for the television series *America's Most Wanted*, she writes three 10-minute music segments per

Carol Nethen

A *multimedia* presentation combines several audio and visual elements.

A *synthesizer* is a computerized electronic instrument that produces and controls sound. It simulates musical instruments and can include rhythm and sound effects.

month. "We work within the same week of broadcast," she says, "sometimes 52 weeks a year."

As a freelancer, Carol is her own boss, planning her daily schedule in order to complete jobs on tight deadlines. Freelancing requires that she work quickly and be able to communicate with her clients. On a typical day, Carol might attend a meeting in Washington, D.C., handle a few business details, and talk on the phone with a client about a long-term project. Her hours are flexible. She may write music at night or early in the morning.

Getting started as a freelance composer had its practical challenges. Carol had to buy state-of-the-art equipment, learn to manage money, and juggle priorities. "I'm a one-person operation, so I do everything."

Carol begins her compositions by watching the video of an upcoming episode on her television monitor. It is connected by software to her computer, so that the music she writes will be in sync—that is, it will exactly fit—with the pictures. She looks for images that inspire musical thoughts. The pacing and subject matter of the video are also important, helping her decide on the rhythm and tone of her music. "The music must breathe with what the pictures are doing. I am never sure about my music until I see the pictures," she says. "In multimedia, I am writing music for emotions and ideas. I love every aspect of that."

Carol also works on several large projects each year. Some jobs, such as composing the music for documentaries or educational films, may take months. And Carol is under

contract with a record company to compose and perform the music for her second album. Like her other projects, making an album has a creative side and a business side. It brings deadlines and hard work. "I work seven days a week," she says, "though there are days when I goof off."

Carol pays close attention to a video of *America's Most Wanted* as she begins to compose at her keyboard.

The Support of a Mentor

Carol's success as a composer didn't happen overnight. For several years after college, she taught music in an elementary school, then at a community college. Feeling dissatisfied with teaching, and wanting more

Carol Nethen

purely creative work, she became interested in composing.

Carol enrolled in a three-year master's program to study music composition and production for film and television. "There were no guarantees I'd be successful," she says. "It was a high-risk investment and I wasn't sure I could do it."

Ever resourceful, Carol found ways to handle the stresses of graduate school. Her worries ranged from making enough money to her most basic fear of not being a good

Becoming a Composer

In addition to film and television sound tracks, *composers* write popular songs and classical, church, and band music. The field is crowded and underpaid, particularly for classical composers. Opportunities are better for composers of church and band music because of the large numbers of church and school choirs and school bands.

Most composers are highly educated, with college degrees in instrumental music or composition. The exceptions are *songwriters,* who sometimes do not have formal education. Many composers also perform.

To prepare for a music-writing career, it's important to play an instrument that allows you to play both harmony and melody. Piano is the best choice, with guitar as another possibility. Electronic keyboards offer the opportunity to write for a variety of instruments.

composer. Fortunately, she found a mentor. "He recognized my talent when no one else did. Now when I write a piece of music, I still ask myself: 'Am I ready to send this to my teacher?' If the answer comes back 'No,' I quickly make the revision." She believes that all aspiring musicians should look for the support an experienced teacher can provide.

After graduate school, Carol's mentor introduced her to the producers at Maryland Public Television. Since the station had no job openings, she offered to become an unpaid intern, knowing she could earn money as a waitress. "It was a wonderful time," she says. "Within three days, my music had gone to tape, and then the show was on television."

After six months, Carol was hired full time as a composer and music producer. At the same time, she was learning to play a synthesizer. Unlike a piano, a synthesizer can electronically simulate other instruments and

It takes a lifetime.

include rhythms and sound effects. It enabled her to write and produce music that sounded almost as if live musicians were playing. Learning to play the synthesizer opened doors for Carol that would have otherwise been closed.

After two years at the television station, her job was eliminated because of budget cuts. Carol then became a freelance composer and producer. Her experience and demo tapes helped her find new clients.

Carol Nethen

The Composer's Moment

Carol would be the first to tell you that being a freelance composer isn't the life for everyone. "It's easy to burn out," she says, "and the isolation can be a problem. You must know when to seek out others." She has learned what works for her. "When I get stuck in my composing, hearing the same things over and over, running on reserves of energy, I need to get together with friends."

Another disadvantage is the uncertainty of making a living. "Not having enough money is devastating. I teach piano one day a week. I could go to five days a week if I needed to." She adds, "There are no composer jobs waiting for you. If you are resourceful enough, you can make a living at it."

Musicians record *demo tapes* to showcase their music.

Choir members rehearse a new piece of music.

Carol believes that a successful composer must learn to work when conditions are not perfect and recognize opportunities that offer experience. Local chamber or choral groups, for example, might be willing to play or sing your compositions, she says. "And if you take a church music job, there is a wonderful

Music Arranging

Arranging music is a related career field. *Arrangers* take a composition and rewrite it for different instruments or voices. Sometimes they change the basic musical style of a composition. Arrangers work for churches, school and military bands, record companies, and film and video companies. Although there is more work available for arrangers than composers, arranging music is still an overcrowded field. The musical background required for an arranger is similar to what is needed for a composer.

opportunity for you to write music."

But if there are drawbacks to being a freelance composer, there are also advantages. Carol tells a story of her early days at the public television station: "I remember a public television documentary. I was conducting the musicians on a piece that I wrote. At the end of the first take, I couldn't speak. They had played the emotion I had written. That moment is the composer's moment."

As for the future, Carol plans to write movie scores or an opera. She is realistic about her chances. "If I have to write 10 movies to do one, I will." Then she laughs. "All those people who get Emmys have gray hair. It takes a lifetime." She adds, "There was no way I could have been a successful composer right out of college. I was still developing."

Kevin Cardiff

Chapter Two

Violin Maker

ost good instruments have at least one wolf," says violin maker Kevin Cardiff. "If they don't, it usually means they don't have much sound either." He is talking about the wolf tones, the "one or two notes on most violins that tend to squawk." He takes a violin off his studio wall to demonstrate.
Violin making is not an art learned overnight, Kevin says, but one that comes slowly with years of experience and repetition. Like playing the violin, violin making takes exceptional patience. "One of the hardest aspects to understand when you first start doing violin making is that knowing how to do it is not enough," he says. "You have to have done it 50 times."

Kevin also repairs and restores violins—filling and retouching cracks, resetting necks, and cutting and replacing bridges on instruments. Each task may take hours of careful work. He puts in long, solitary days, sometimes going down to his shop late at night to add another coat of varnish to an instrument.

Making a violin requires different skills, including choosing and cutting the wood, carving the wood to just the right thickness, then gluing the parts together and varnishing the instrument. But it is not enough to be a fine woodworker. Kevin emphasizes that a violin maker has to be sensitive to the individual sound of each instrument and the needs of the player.

A *bridge* is the small piece of wood on the front of a violin that supports the strings and carries their vibrations to the body of the instrument.

The long narrow piece of wood extending from the body of a violin is called the *neck.*

It takes him well over 150 hours to make each violin. Unlike many violin makers, Kevin does most of the work by hand. "This is something I really love and feel like I'm doing it for me. When it's done and I'm happy about it, I'm really proud."

A Second Career

Kevin is a concert violinist turned violin maker. Having given up his symphony career after 17 years, he talks like a man who has thought a lot about his choices. He has. Once musicians win an audition with a major symphony orchestra, they rarely leave before retirement. That's why there are so few orchestra openings and the competition for them is so fierce.

But Kevin is an exception. Because of a childhood fascination with violins, he found himself repairing instruments for his fellow musicians in the Baltimore Symphony. During summer vacations, he took courses in violin making and repair. Kevin then apprenticed himself to a well-known violin maker. For

Members of the viola, cello, and bass sections perform in a symphony orchestra.

Kevin Cardiff

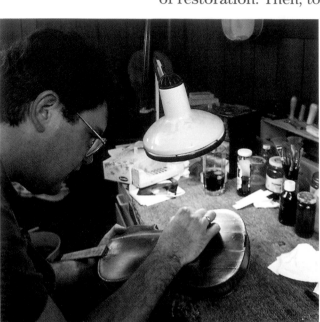

Kevin works on a violin in his shop.

four years, he spent one afternoon a month with his teacher, learning the techniques of restoration. Then, to test-drive his new career, he took a leave of absence from the symphony with the understanding that he could return. He never did.

Looking back, Kevin has few regrets, although he sometimes misses the companionship of fellow musicians. "I really enjoy having my own sense of accomplishment," he says. He points to the unfinished violins he plans to complete when he takes a break from the repair and restoration work. "If I make a violin and I'm happy with it, it's mine. I really did something. In a symphony orchestra, especially if you're a string player, you don't really have individual accomplishment."

Kevin is also grateful for the control he has over his work life, something he never had playing with an orchestra. "Most of your playing is done on holidays, evenings, and weekends because you're the entertainment—and that's when people want to be entertained." Now he works when he wants to, at his own pace. "My business hours are 9:30 to 5:30 by appointment. And if

I feel like taking a month off, I can do it as long as I have enough money."

But if Kevin's new lifestyle has certain advantages, it also has drawbacks. "There's always a certain amount of risk and uncertainty about being self-employed," he

> ## If I make a violin and I'm happy with it, it's mine. I really did something.

says. "You don't really know what your income's going to be." And then there is the paperwork, which he dislikes. "But what I hate most is people who don't take care of their instruments. And I would say the most difficult aspect of this business and any business is difficult people."

A Musical Life

Kevin grew up in a large family of amateur musicians in Pennsylvania. At age 10, he enrolled in a free summer violin class. Soon he was taking private lessons. In high school, he became the concertmaster—the lead violinist—of the school orchestra. Twice, the local musician's union paid his way to the national Congress of Strings, an annual conference for young string players.

After graduation, Kevin studied first at the New School of Music in Philadelphia, transferring to the Eastman School of Music

Kevin Cardiff

in Rochester, New York, a year later. He played for the Rochester Philharmonic until graduation. A graduate degree at Yale University and a job with the New Haven Symphony were next.

Then he was invited to audition for the Baltimore Symphony. "One of my downfalls always was nerves, not so much in performance but in auditions," he says. "The Baltimore Symphony audition took place all in one day. I played four times, because they had me play preliminaries and semifinals, then play a solo piece, then do some sight-reading of music I hadn't practiced. I was there from 9 A.M. until 8 P.M." Kevin was one of three violinists who auditioned that day. Today, he says, close to three hundred people would audition for the job. "It's insane," he says.

Kevin plays one of the violins he has made.

The Future

Kevin played with the Baltimore Symphony for 12 years. He still performs occasionally but now is fully committed to his violin-making career. Four years ago, he had 30 regular clients. Now he has 300 and a growing national reputation.

In the future, Kevin says, he hopes to have more time to make and restore violins. "It is very gratifying to find a fine old instrument and bring it back to great condition." When a wealthy violin collector died last year, Kevin restored the entire collection of 30 instruments so they could be put up for auction.

He cautions against future violin makers giving up repair and restoration work, which still makes up three-quarters of his business: "In the next 10 or 12 years there are going to be a lot of good violin makers. A lot of them don't want to do repairs, so they will starve." Larger cities with orchestras, he says, can always use good violin repairers.

Kevin's advice to anyone interested in violin making is first to learn to play at least at an intermediate level. Kevin believes his clients trust him because of his years as a performer. "I know that even $\frac{1}{32}$ or $\frac{1}{64}$ of an inch of extra wood or space between the strings will not feel right to the player," he says.

After learning to play, Kevin says, "Seek out a master violin maker to learn firsthand." He believes violin-making schools can be valuable, too, although he worries that they sometimes turn out "talented woodworkers" who are unable to understand the needs of the players. Kevin still sees his teacher for an occasional afternoon of shop talk. He believes the learning process never ends.

Chuck Redd

Chapter Three

JAZZ
DRUMMER

laying for keeps" is how jazz drummer Chuck Redd describes a recording session. "It's high-pressure work for a musician," he says. "A lot of money is at stake. If you are having a bad day, you definitely have to keep it to yourself."

Chuck has done 20 recordings, most of them with the legendary jazz guitarist Charlie Byrd and Charlie's brother, bass player Joe Byrd. First they discuss the music. Then they schedule a rehearsal to read through the songs. As a drummer, Chuck creates the drum part using the music from the melody or the bass part. Rhythms are especially important: "I have either the trumpet or bass or piano part. I have to know how to respond and react."

When recording day arrives, Chuck is ready. "The concentration level is high. First you play without the microphone. Then you turn it on and everyone usually tenses up," he says with a smile.

Making a recording takes at least two long, exhausting days. There can be equipment failures. And since musicians wear headphones to hear the recording, they often cannot hear their own natural sound or each other. "It is very demanding, both emotionally and physically," Chuck says. "Your state of mind has to be perfect."

Recording is only a small part of Chuck's work. Since he performs in the evening, often playing well past midnight, he keeps his hours flexible in order to be rested for the next performance. In addition to practicing during the day, he often listens to recordings and schedules performances.

Hard Work and a Dash of Luck

Chuck's first memory is of dancing to a Louis Armstrong album from his father's jazz and big-band collection. He began to take drum lessons when he was 10, about the time he met Charlie Byrd, a friend of his family.

"I loved Charlie's music, with its Brazilian and bossa nova rhythms. He was unique. No one else was playing jazz on classical guitar. I'd get to sit in with him. I knew all the arrangements. My goal," Chuck says, "was to play with Charlie. My father told me not to shoot too high, but I thought to myself: 'I'm going to do it.'"

Chuck took lessons, practiced up to eight hours a day, and listened endlessly to the music of America's most famous jazz musicians. By high school graduation, he was playing professionally. When he was 21, luck smiled: Charlie Byrd needed a drummer. That was 14 years ago.

As part of the Charlie Byrd Trio, Chuck has worked and toured with some of the best jazz musicians in the world. The highlight of his career, he says, has been to "play with musicians I listened to on records as I was growing up."

Chuck performs with the Charlie Byrd Trio.

On the Road

Although Chuck still performs as part of the Charlie Byrd Trio, he does other work as well. As a member of the Smithsonian Jazz Masterworks Orchestra, he plays concerts in cities around the country. He also does independent gigs in New York a couple of days a month. All told, his travel schedule takes him away from home two to five months a year. To practice, says Chuck, "I carry a pair of sticks and brushes and play on phone books and pray we don't get thrown out of the hotel."

Touring takes Chuck to foreign countries with appreciative audiences, but it is also stressful. "Scheduling doesn't allow for enough sleep. You get quick meals or no meals," he says. "You must get up and perform for a lot of people who have waited to hear you for a long time."

Chuck describes a recent tour to Europe. It included a missed flight, three canceled concerts, a last-minute recording session with no rehearsal time, plus days of waiting and

A club gig requires Chuck's full concentration.

The Charlie Byrd Trio

wondering what would come next. At the end of the two weeks, there was a frantic race to get back to New York in time to perform at the Village Vanguard, a celebrated jazz club. Chuck managed it, with about half an hour to spare. "If you aren't serious and dedicated enough, you won't make it," he says.

When Chuck is at home, he maintains his three-hour daily practice schedule and plays in local concerts. "People assume what we do is somehow easier because the hours we work are shorter. What they don't realize is that you must spend many more hours practicing."

The Business of Music

Like many musicians, Chuck regards the business side of his life as a necessary evil. He must contact the concert promoters, booking agents, and other musicians who hire him. Although he has not yet needed an agent or business manager, Chuck knows he will need one when he is ready to record a solo album or form his own group—both long-term goals. "Self-promotion," he says, "is difficult for a lot of musicians. It takes away from musical preparation and practice time. But you have to barrel ahead and do it."

Your Foot in the Door

"Luck gets your foot in the door," says Chuck, "but you must live up to expectations. You are expected to get better and better." He believes that there is no such thing as a typical career in jazz. "Figure out what you truly love. Become as good a musician as you can become. The financial rewards aren't great necessarily."

"It also helps," he says, "to get along with people and respect other musicians. Let them know that they can trust you. You need to be punctual and responsible and play at a certain level, regardless of fatigue and financial difficulties."

Chuck also thinks that listening is "a big part of being a jazz musician. Know the history of jazz. You need to listen to your peers and to the people who came before you. And you need to listen to yourself. It's the hardest thing to listen to your own recordings. You may think that a recording is good and then you hear that it isn't good. It's educational."

Luck gets your foot in the door, but you must live up to expectations. You are expected to get better and better.

If Chuck has any regret, it is that he dropped out of college after two and a half years to play full time. "You should go to school and become well-rounded. You need good early training." He stresses the importance of good teachers.

As for the future of jazz, Chuck is not completely optimistic. "There is much less work now. The level of musicianship is higher, but there is not as much personality in playing." But love for the music keeps Chuck going. "I love playing for an audience which is responding and knowledgeable," he says. "You can't become a jazz musician for the wrong reasons: money, travel, fame, or prestige. You become a jazz musician because you truly love to play the music."

Debra Blount

Chapter Four

ARTS ADMINISTRATOR

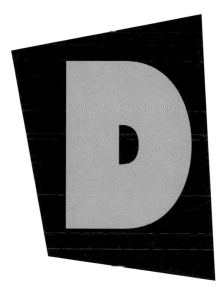

Debra Blount's office at The Washington Opera is too small. Her desk is nearly lost between boxes of magazines and programs. There are shelves crammed with books, posters leaning against the wall, even costumes hung behind the door. As education and community programs director, she is in the middle of planning programs for next year. Her tiny office is in the Kennedy Center for the Performing Arts where The Washington Opera makes its home.

A Way with People

Debra's job requires hard work, creativity, a cool head to handle unexpected emergency situations, and perhaps, most of all, a way with people. "I can talk to anybody," she says.

And that's important. A typical day might find her meeting with her huge staff of volunteers, negotiating with singers, or coordinating the "Artists in the Schools" program with local teachers. After 5:00, she may attend opera social events, performances, or meetings with volunteers.

Unlike many administrators, she says, "I even like the fund-raising side. You can't develop wonderful programs without money." Debra describes her meetings with The Washington Opera's sponsors. "They appreciate opera, so I can talk with them about it."

Getting Started

Only a few years ago, Debra was singing in theatrical productions in high school. "But I realized that there weren't many opportunities in musical theater for African-American women," she says. So when a teacher suggested her soprano voice gave her the potential for a career as an opera singer, she decided to major in vocal performance at Catholic University. It was during college that she saw her first opera. Since then she has seen nearly 150 more.

After graduation Debra took a nonmusical job as a provider services representative with a health care firm. "I persuaded them that because of all my music training, I was good at communicating with people," she says. "My parents were both in the health care industry, too, and I knew a lot of the vocabulary."

In the meantime, she continued to study independently. "I went to the library and took out opera records," she says. "I listened to three a week. My goal was to save money, study voice, practice, and learn about opera." In order to know people in the field and gain experience, she volunteered at Opera America, an organization that promotes opera throughout the United States. "But I

Arts Administration

Full-time and part-time *arts administrators* work for orchestras, opera and ballet companies, theaters, and large private or government-funded arts organizations. They are the behind-the-scenes people who make the show go on: from the *ushers* and *ticket office personnel* to the *accountants, fund-raisers, education directors, marketing and public relations people,* all the way up to the *general managers.* Many have experience as performers and all work long hours and are often underpaid. Education—in music, dance, theater, arts administration, liberal arts, or business administration—is valuable, but on-the-job training and professional contacts are the most important.

knew that at age 24 I could still become a singer if I wanted," she says.

Opera America suggested that Debra consider opera administration as a career. They encouraged her to apply for one of their three annual fellowships for a yearlong program to train opera administrators.

She applied, was accepted, and began an educational adventure that would eventually take her across the country to three very different opera companies: the Dallas Opera, the Lyric Opera of Kansas City, and the Chautauqua Opera in upstate New York. Over the year, she made professional friends she still values. Contacts, she says, are important in the small world of opera and arts administration.

But more important, something else happened. "I stopped singing. And you know what?" she asks. "I didn't miss it at all. I was relieved. I just knew singing was not for me. I

I can talk to anybody.

wasn't willing to make the sacrifices."

Debra recognized that her career was headed toward arts administration, probably with an opera company. Wisely, she had stayed in touch with opera friends in Washington during her fellowship year. Within weeks of returning to Washington, she was offered a full-time job as assistant to the administrative director at The Washington Opera. Nine months later, she became the first education and community programs director.

The Season

Debra divides the year into halves: the Season, from November through April when The Washington Opera is performing and the educational programs are in high gear—and the Off-Season, from May though October when there are no performances and she has time to plan. Hers is a demanding job, one that often consumes her evenings and weekends, particularly during the Season. "I want to do so much, but there are not enough financial or human resources," she says. "And I hate doing things that take me away from developing programs." But it's hard to

Students perform in the Washington Opera's "Opera Camp."

As part of the "Look In" program, Debra and singers from *Madame Butterfly* speak to children in the audience after a performance.

believe that there is much about her job she doesn't like. "I have the best job in the company," she says.

Debra describes herself as a "mini-general manager who does a little of what is done in every other department in the opera." Within her department, she wears many hats: fund-raiser, program developer and administrator, budget director, volunteer coordinator, and marketing executive. Keeping within her budget, she creates educational and entertaining programs to bring to local schools and the community. Then to make them happen, she hires artists, trains volunteers, and makes all the practical arrangements. One example is the "Look In" program, which brings students behind the scenes to watch a performance with full orchestra at The Washington Opera.

The Arts in the 21st Century

Although Debra freely admits that it can be difficult to find a job in opera or arts administration, she says, "The arts will always be with us. There is always going to be a need to get people involved in the arts." She believes that the future will bring more partnerships between opera and the other arts. "You can be an expert in one area, but learn about other areas as well." A college degree is necessary, either in one of the arts, such as music or dance, or in liberal arts, business, or arts administration.

Describing her own career path as "fairly typical," Debra stresses work experience. "Volunteering is often the only opportunity to get experience. And you need experience to get a job," she says. "I would welcome young volunteers here."

As for her own future, she is optimistic. "I am thinking about going to graduate school to get my masters in business administration," she says. It will give her better management skills. In the meantime, Debra is doing a job that "combines love of opera with love of people. Even though we have limited space, I'm where I need to be. I want to make opera accessible to everyone." She feels strongly about making a difference. "Sometimes," she says, "we lose sight of what's really important. That's developing the soul and the spirit."

Doug Forbes

Chapter Five

Music Teacher and Church Musician

t's another of July's dog days, hot and sticky outside, cool and pleasant in the church basement. Music teacher and church organist Doug Forbes has begun his relaxed summer schedule. This is when he plans his church music programs for the rest of the year, reading music catalogs and ordering music. He may also arrange music to meet the needs of his volunteer choir. "I try to keep the music fresh Sunday after Sunday," he says.

For 10 months of the year Doug is not just a church musician but a full-time music teacher in a private school. During the school year, his schedule is so hectic he rarely has much time for himself and his family. Four days a week, he gives private piano lessons after a full day of classroom teaching. On Thursday afternoons, he practices organ at the church and then holds a two-hour rehearsal with the choir in the evening. On Sunday mornings, he rehearses the choir one last time before the service.

That Goose-Bumpy Feeling

Doug's interest in music began early. And it began in a church: the awe-inspiring National Cathedral in Washington, D.C., with its splendid organ and renowned Men and Boys' Choir. He became a choirboy when he was eight. "The National Cathedral was one of the grander places for hearing and making music in the world," he says. "I realized that music was something I couldn't live without. Once you get that goose-bumpy feeling, you try to capture it again throughout your life."

It was during high school that Doug became interested in classical orchestral

The National Cathedral's Men and Boys' Choir performs in the cathedral.

music. He played the trumpet and the piano. And he fell in love with the music of the Beatles, the Rolling Stones, and the Beach Boys. "I loved all kinds of music," he says. "There wasn't a bit of it I preferred over any other." At 16 he was chosen as the first student guest conductor of the U.S. Air Force Band. This experience opened up the world of conducting. "Bit by bit," he says, "I was sucked into the whole spectrum of music."

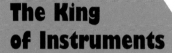

The King of Instruments

At the New England Conservatory in Boston, Doug decided to major in organ. "I wanted the orchestral sound without having to worry about 80 musicians. They call the organ the "King of Instruments." I fell in love with how powerful it was. It was the synthesizer of its time."

A highlight of his college years was conducting a concert of symphonic and rock music at Symphony Hall, home of the Boston Symphony Orchestra and the famed Boston Pops. Ninety musicians, from rock bands and music schools, brought the house down. Doug remembers it as "a once-in-a-lifetime concert."

By college graduation, Doug was working as assistant organist at the Church of the Advent, a job he kept while completing a master's degree at Boston Conservatory. When a position opened up for a music teacher at the church school, he jumped at the chance. "That's how I came to fall in love with teaching."

Doug practices the organ.

with Teaching

Doug has never fallen
out of love with
teaching. After
many years, he
still finds teaching rewarding.
He admits he's very lucky to teach at a school
where music is appreciated. "The performing

Teaching Opportunities

There are more jobs in music education than in any other music profession. Full-time jobs exist in schools, colleges, and universities. In addition, many *teachers* give private lessons. Teaching jobs require at least four years of college, usually in music education or vocal or instrumental music. Teachers of instrumental music must learn how to play many different instruments. In addition, to teach in a public school, a teacher must be certified by the state. Each state has its own requirements, including education courses, tests, and student teaching. Teaching in private or parochial schools usually does not require certification. Nor does college teaching, which is, however, a very crowded field. To teach at a college level, you will need at least a master's degree if not a doctorate in music.

arts are visible here. People give money in support. They understand that the arts play a part in the growth of a person."

Doug describes a new arts center at Roland Park Country School where he teaches. He has big dreams for music. "I want to get other local schools involved, to get

Teaching is never boring. For me it's a perfect life.

together a community orchestra. I want to give parents and kids the chance to perform with professional musicians."

"Teaching," Doug says, "is never boring. For me it's a perfect life, loving music and children like I do." But Doug also recognizes that not all teachers work in communities that are so sympathetic to the arts. He doesn't know how most music teachers remain as dedicated as they do. He also admits that "classroom teaching doesn't pay a whole lot of money, which is another reason I have the church job and do private teaching."

What Makes a Good Teacher?

Doug has given a lot of thought to what makes a good teacher. "To teach, you have to be unselfish," he says. "You have to be secure enough to give someone else a chance. You have to give up some of your own music making to other people who want to learn. It's a hard thing to do."

His advice to people who plan to teach music is to first "get comfortable with the technique on your instrument. It requires hours of practice. And you have to take all opportunities to perform." Doug also thinks that "hands-on experience working with children" is valuable. In addition to school music activities and private lessons, he suggests community and church-based programs. "If music is your passion, you will begin to find possibilities in these places."

As for the future of teaching music, Doug thinks that new technology is already changing things. "With the software and synthesizers, it's incredibly exciting. A lot of the mundane tasks are gone. But," he says, "in many ways teaching music will remain the same. Pianos will still have the same 88 keys. And good teachers will still want to work with children."

Church Music

Like most church musicians, Doug works part time, in addition to his full-time teaching. He plays the organ, rehearses and directs the church choir, and plans all of the musical activities for the church. "You need a ton of flexibility. I can't always do the music I want," he says, describing the limited availability of the singers. Sometimes there are not enough singers on a part, and sometimes the singers haven't the time to learn the music quickly enough to sing it the next Sunday morning.

"I also wish I could spend more time here. Church music is very exciting. There are opportunities for arranging and conducting

Sacred Music

Most church music jobs are part time. Sometimes musicians have more than one church job, which can make for a hectic weekend schedule as they dash from one service to another. Most *church musicians* are broadly trained in music, with experience as *choir directors, arrangers,* and *organists.* There are also a few freelance jobs for *singers* and *instrumentalists,* particularly string and brass players.

Some larger churches and synagogues have full-time *music directors* or *organists* on staff. No specific education is required, but most church musicians are highly educated.

and composing and performing. Unfortunately, they are less than there used to be. And there is the money angle always. I would like to be able to think less about it." Then he pauses. "Church musicians are very creative," he says. With small budgets and volunteer choirs, they have to be.

Victor Giordano

Chapter Six

RECORDING ENGINEER

'm not technical, not technical at all," says recording engineer Victor Giordano. It's hard to believe that when you look around Clean Cuts studio. "I can't fix any of this stuff," he adds, waving his hand at the computer that controls the audio and video. Beyond the equipment is the tiny enclosed glass recording studio where live musicians play during recording sessions. Victor remembers his first recording venture. He was nine. Using two tape recorders, he made a primitive multitrack recording, adding music and vocals in the background. It was a fitting beginning.

Today he records on 24 tracks, using a mixture of live instruments, sound effects, and other musical elements generated by synthesizers. Each track adds another layer of sound or a different instrument. Victor must pay attention to rhythm and timing, judge the sound as it goes along, and make small adjustments to improve

Victor adjusts a microphone before a recording session.

the overall balance. Later, the tracks will be edited and blended into the final recording or put to pictures for television commercials, films, or documentaries.

As senior engineer and part owner of Clean Cuts, Victor is in the studio only on the days he is recording. Although the studio tries for a 10:00 A.M. to 6:00 P.M. workday, a session will often start in the afternoon and go late into the evening. Odd hours are more likely during album recording sessions than when making commercials for television. "Ad agencies keep business hours," he says. He still occasionally works weekends, but summer holidays are slow.

Timing and Rhythm

Victor grew up listening to Elvis Presley and the Beatles, wanting to be part of "the next supergroup," he says. He began guitar lessons at age seven. By his teens, he was playing guitar and bass with several rock bands. When he was 20, one band "got backing for an album, enough money to record in a 24-track studio in

Boston." He was instantly hooked on sound engineering. "I knew it was for me."

Victor still occasionally plays bass for record album projects, although he no longer performs live for audiences. But he is grateful

> ## If you don't play an instrument, talk to musicians, listen to all kinds of music. You need tolerance for all kinds and styles.

for his musical background. "It gave me timing and rhythm. You can't imagine how important rhythm is to a recording engineer." And because he is a musician, he says his clients trust his judgment.

Although Victor attended college at the urging of his parents, he dropped out to learn sound engineering. As luck would have it, an innovator in modern sound recording had just opened a studio near his home.

"I went to that studio," Victor says with a laugh, "and I begged. I said that I'd do anything. They let me stay. It was my training. For a year or more I was strictly a volunteer. I made money playing in bands and as a studio musician."

When the recording studio relocated to a barge in Baltimore Harbor, Victor helped build it. Then the barge sank. "We lost a nine-foot Steinway [piano] and vintage guitars and

Victor Giordano

many tapes." That night, when a local television station reported the story, Victor was identified as a professional recording engineer, not as the trainee he really was. The next day, a call came from another studio. "They said 'I guess you need a job.' I said, 'I guess I do.'" So he was hired for the first time as an engineer. "I had to wing it," he says.

Other Recording Careers

Many recording projects need the services of other specialists. These people are often *freelancers* who are well paid for the hours they work.

A *sound designer* is a specialist who blends instruments and sound effects to create a combination of sounds for television or radio commercials. A *record-mastering technician* makes the final adjustments to an album—putting the songs in order, adjusting dynamic range, and equalizing the sound. A *producer* is another pair of ears, hired by the recording artists or the studio to oversee the recording session.

"Coming out of that famous studio, they thought I knew more than I did."

Since then Victor has worked for a number of studios. He likes best the pure "music engineering," in which albums are recorded as musicians play live.

But "production engineering" is the bread-and-butter work for most sound studios. Calling their work "mix to pix," production engineers put elements of music together with sound effects, then add the visuals to make television commercials.

Victor describes a commercial starring Baltimore Oriole Cal Ripkin. Kettle drums, the boom of a flash from an old-fashioned camera, and a hand grenade were used as the audio backdrop for a picture of a baseball scoreboard. "A scoreboard makes no noise," Victor says. "We made a noise." His studio has a sound library of thousands of sound effects on hundreds of compact discs.

Learn to Listen

A sense of calm pervades the Clean Cuts studio. Victor emphasizes that being "laid back" is important for an engineer. "You must not get flustered," he says. "You must work quickly, but you can't be sloppy either." And then there are the last-minute changes and revisions. "It happens all the time. There is no use getting upset about it."

A sound engineer has to learn to listen, Victor says, and he doesn't just mean to the music. Victor has to listen to his clients. He has to know when to offer an opinion. "It's best to lay back sometimes," he says. "You have to be honest and professional."

The Rewards

Victor says the most gratifying part of his job is working with all kinds of music. "It widens my scope. We do reggae and rap, classical, rock, and country. I appreciate it all." Although he likes recording albums, he also likes seeing the results of his work fast. "A commercial is done quickly, and you see it on the air." But with either music or production engineering, the end result is always what counts. "The hardest part to accept," he says, "is that it could have been better."

Rapidly Changing Technology

Victor's advice for future sound engineers? Find a way to get on-the-job experience. "Get involved in school audio projects. Record school plays or musicals." He suggests looking at *Mix Magazine* to find names of local studios that might take volunteers. "And if you don't play an instrument, talk to musicians, listen to all kinds of music. You need tolerance for all kinds and styles."

He also mentions the audio engineering programs now offered by colleges. "Knowledge of computers is essential. Everything here is computer driven." He points to an 80-channel console run by computer. "Digitalized phone lines can hook up other studios all around the country. We can do sessions from anywhere. You wouldn't believe how fast the technology is changing."

Victor looks forward to doing more pure music engineering. And he hopes to continue

to build the reputation of Clean Cuts, which is just two years old. Big-name clients from around the country will improve the chances for the studio's continued financial success. But when asked about a move to one of the big recording towns—New York or Los Angeles or Nashville—Victor shakes his head. "I'm happy right here." Current technology will let him work as if he were in one of those cities anyway.

Victor makes adjustments during a recording session.

Lisa Simeone

Chapter Seven

DISC JOCKEY

listen to music all day long, so at home I listen to silence," says classical disc jockey and public radio commentator Lisa Simeone. In addition to playing recorded music, she also tapes interviews with writers, musicians, economists, scientists, architects, and political activists. Her shift at WJHU in Baltimore begins at 1:00 in the afternoon and ends after she does the local announcements for National Public Radio's show *All Things Considered* at 6:30.

What the Audience Doesn't See

Although Lisa's audience may picture her listening to Bach along with them, she's not. On a typical day, she is interviewing guests, editing previous interviews for the air, choosing music for the next day, and lining up future interviews by telephone.

As you watch her work, you notice a natural rhythm that comes from experience. Some sixth sense tells her when a piece of music is about to end. "It's essential to think on your feet," she says. Asked about on-air bloopers, she laughs: "Hiccups. It happens once in a blue moon, right before you turn the mike on. You try to get on and get off."

Lisa also announces live concerts, often for the Baltimore Symphony Orchestra. "I'm under the stage looking at a tiny television monitor." She has also accompanied the symphony to Europe, doing two radio reports a day. "I was scared to death, but it was successful."

Since public radio stations are supported by listeners' donations, her job also has a fund-raising side. "It's a major and difficult part of my job," she says. Another of Lisa's off-air responsibilities is to make appearances at events the station supports. "I recognize it is part of my job, but I'm more particular now. I don't say yes to everything." The requests for public appearances, she says, can lead to burnout if you don't pace yourself.

Babysitting CDs

Lisa's career as a DJ began as a volunteer at a tiny community college radio station. After graduating with a liberal arts degree from St. John's College in Annapolis, she knew that she had to find a way to get more experience for a career as a DJ. "The community college station gave me three hours a week," she says. Within months she

landed a full-time job at a Baltimore classical music station. Two years later, it was on to another station, this time in Washington. Now she is back in Baltimore.

Her early radio work was mostly what she calls "babysitting CDs," the record spinning that people associate with being a DJ. But she also learned how to use the equipment to edit tape, a favorite task. Today editing tape is a "dying art," she says, because stations have gone digital, and tape is rarely used.

The Voice

Lisa's radio career sounds like it was made for her—especially when you hear her voice. "The voice was always there," she says. "Teachers chose me to do narrations in school." And although she performed in high school plays and musicals, she didn't develop her love and

It's essential to think on your feet.

knowledge of music until her years at St. John's College.

If Lisa's voice was ideal, so was her natural gift for broadcasting. "To talk about music was easy. I had a knack for it," she says. "You either have it or you don't. You are either engaging or boring, animated or dull." With experience, she has allowed her own personality to shine through. "You have to be friendly on the air. You have to be down-to-earth and spontaneous. I pride myself on

sounding correct, just not pretentious or pompous."

The Music

As for the music itself, Lisa plays mostly classical works, instrumental and choral, choosing from a large library at the station. She recalls her first jobs. "I chose my own music, and I used to do a ton of research." Now she does a lot less. "There are about five hundred classical basics," she says. "I try to mix it up: some classical, some baroque, some romantic, some early music." Some afternoons she plays listener requests. "But it's my own taste to some degree."

Lisa admits that she has more freedom and flexibility than many other public radio DJs. "I won't play whole operas," she says, "but I will play songs, choral works, cantatas." She also plays some folk and international music.

Public versus Commercial Radio

There are important differences between public and commercial radio stations, she points out. In commercial radio, "many DJs have no personal choices," she says. "They have a playlist." And although there may be more room for creativity in public radio, she admits that commercial DJs get paid better. On the down side, DJs often have less job security in the commercial markets, where formats change frequently to keep up with audience and advertisers' tastes. One month it's jazz, the next it may be country and western programming.

Music on the Radio

Radio stations are either commercial—supported by on-air advertising—or public—supported by donations from listeners, corporations, and foundations. There are many more commercial stations, most of them playing some combination of rock and roll, rap, jazz, folk, Top 40, oldies, and country-and-western music. Public stations tend toward classical or jazz programming, sometimes both.

Depending on the size of the station, decisions about what kind of music to play are made by either a *program director* or a *music director.* At larger stations, the program director selects and schedules the programs, including news shows, such as National Public Radio's *All Things Considered,* which is heard nationwide. The music director makes up the station's general playlist, listens to new releases, does market research on what the public is listening to, and even fills in for ailing *DJs.* In small stations, one person will do all of these tasks.

Lisa Simeone

Ironically, WJHU is also changing, from an all classical music format to a format with many more talk shows. Lisa will now host a talk show on Sunday mornings plus the Baltimore Symphony Orchestra series. In addition to other freelance projects, she will also produce features for National Public Radio's *All Things Considered* and *Morning Edition.*

Lisa gets ready to go live on the air.

The Studio

Like all DJs, Lisa works in a small studio surrounded by an intimidating array of equipment. In addition to the satellite feeds, which pick up broadcasts anywhere in the world, a computer allows her to punch up the current weather conditions to share with her audience.

"You don't need to study to learn how to run the equipment," she says. "You can learn it on the job." She also discourages students from enrolling at technical schools. "Get a general education," she advises. "Be well-read. Be interested." To learn the technical side, she suggests getting an internship. "Volunteer. Be willing to work for free," she says. "Besides, it's fun to hang around stations."

The Future of Radio

As for the future of radio, Lisa is upbeat. "Radio is portable and small," she says. "You can take it with you, in the car, the boat, the shower." As for the technology, she says that satellite feeds and numerous cable channels will increase listeners' choices. "There's a lot of automation, but people are always going to want creative thought to listen to. Someone will always have to be there to send it."

Kevin Sullivan

Chapter Eight

CHILD LIFE SPECIALIST

hild life specialist Kevin Sullivan uses music to reach disabled or sick children who might not otherwise respond. He is in training to become a music therapist, a career that combines music and psychology.

"Being in the hospital is rough for a child," he says. "We try to create an environment which is safe and expressive." And Kevin, with his tambourines, wood blocks, and guitar also offers moments of joy. "If anything surprised me about this, it's how a sick kid can get enjoyment out of music. The mood in the room changes when you begin singing."

A Typical Work Day

A typical day for Kevin starts before 8:00 A.M., as he reviews his schedule, writes down the patients' progress on their charts, and thinks about his goals for each individual or group session he will conduct. Music therapists, he notes, do more than just use music as recreation. They have specific goals for each patient or group of patients.

Kevin tries to find the most appropriate way to use music. For example, if he is working with a child who has trouble paying attention, his goal might be as simple as getting the child to "follow directions."

Using music, Kevin might ask the child to play a drum while he plays the keyboard, giving encouragement when the child responds.

Kevin also tries to find instruments that please each child, whether they be drums, keyboards, or his guitar. "You have to be really creative," he says. He once taped sticks of wood to a child's hands so that the child could bang and play by himself. "Music gives kids a sense of mastery and control of their environment," Kevin says.

Kevin also finds he needs to shift gears often. "You need a ton of flexibility to work with children," he says. At any given time, he works with about six individual patients. In addition, he leads small and large groups.

He uses the computer with some children, operating special music software. He explains that children who don't have much control over their bodies can still push a mouse or use a special keyboard. One of his

Music Therapy

To be hired as a *music therapist,* you must be either registered by the National Association for Music Therapy or certified by the American Association for Music Therapy. Although slightly different, both professional organizations set requirements for education and clinical training. Both recommend music therapy programs—undergraduate and graduate—at certain colleges and universities. Most music therapists work in nursing or retirement homes, in hospitals, or in special schools. Salaries are roughly equivalent to those of public school *music teachers* and depend on experience and education.

future goals is to write music software for disabled children.

Kevin's Career Path

Although he came from a nonmusical family, Kevin began playing the piano at age four. He studied piano and saxophone during his school years, playing in a high school jazz ensemble. After graduation he toured Europe with the Youth of America Concert Band and String Orchestra. "But I wanted to be a rock-and-roll star like everyone else," he says. He went on to major in music education at Berklee College of Music in Boston.

Kevin's first job after college was teaching music in a public school in Massachusetts. That job disappeared when the school budget was cut. He found himself without work, living aimlessly at the beach, wondering about his future.

Kevin soon developed a plan to create a career as a private teacher. Within a year, he had 60 students and was teaching guitar, piano, flute, and saxophone at a rented studio space. Studio teaching left him with some free time, so he began taking psychology courses at local colleges. And he volunteered at a school for children with disabilities, helping the kids put on *The Sound of Music*. It was a summer that changed his career focus. "The kids with disabilities," he says, "have taught me so much."

When the summer was over, Kevin volunteered again, this time at the children's hospital where he now works. Within months, a job opened up for an assistant in the Child Life Department. Soon Kevin's new supervisor recommended him for a four-month internship at Johns Hopkins Medical School, where he could gain more experience. He was assigned to the pediatric (children's) intensive care and cancer units.

Kevin's experience working with very sick children now qualifies him to work with doctors and therapists as a member of the

I get to go home at night and know I made a difference in a kid's life.

professional team, using music to help the children express or enjoy themselves. And he is well on his way to completing the supervised practical experience he needs to become a registered music therapist.

Making a Difference

Kevin knows exactly why he does what he does. "I get to go home at night and know I made a difference in a kid's life." It's great, he says, when the "kids are up and dancing, grabbing wheelchairs and spinning other kids around, even the ones in beds or on stretchers. I love when the kids get goofy and happy."

But working with disabled children has a difficult side. Kevin admits he has trouble accepting that the children he works with often have only a limited time to live. "Death

Kevin Sullivan

is going to happen, but it strikes really hard," he says.

A Career in Music Therapy

Music therapy is a developing field. There are several ways to become qualified to work

A child joins Kevin as he plays tambourine.

as a music therapist. The most direct path is to study at one of the colleges that offers approved courses and clinical experience. Kevin's more indirect route involved a college degree in another field and on-the-job experience in a supervised program.

Kevin's future is looking bright. His short-term goal is to complete the clinical requirements to become a registered music therapist. Long-term goals include a master's degree, then a doctorate, in psychology. Both will prepare him for a private practice working with children outside a hospital setting.

As for finding out if music therapy is for you, Kevin suggests volunteering at a summer camp, hospital, or nursing home. And then there's the music side. A music therapist needs to sing and play a number of instruments, including piano and percussion. But most important, Kevin believes, is a "mellow personality and unbelievable patience."

Maggie Sansone

Chapter Nine

FOLK MUSICIAN AND RECORD COMPANY EXECUTIVE

'm a musical instrument addict," says Maggie Sansone. She shows off her latest find: a bagpipe called a Scottish small pipe. She also plays piano, banjo, classical and folk guitar, mandolin, recorder, bassoon, bongos, xylophone, pennywhistle, a hand drum called the dombek, and most important to her career, the hammered dulcimer.

It was in Key West that she first came across the hammered dulcimer, an ancient 70-stringed instrument. The player hits the strings with a mallet, which makes the dulcimer sound a bit like a harpsichord.

The dulcimer replaced the guitar as her main instrument. "People who listened to me on the street were really fascinated by it, and since I loved it and it has this wonderful sound, I adopted it."

Maggie's Music

Maggie is the owner of Maggie's Music, a small record label for folk and New Age music. In addition she performs, records albums, and writes instruction books.

The Record Business

Maggie's Music is a small independent record company. Although there are many such companies, they almost always specialize in one kind of music. Most records, particularly those showcasing famous performers, are produced by huge corporations with vast resources. New York, Los Angeles, and Nashville are hubs of record making.

A career in a large record company is quite different from Maggie's career. Jobs in large companies are specialized and may require a background in business, law, marketing and public relations, computers, or graphics, rather than in music.

Having a traditional job was never Maggie's goal. She laughs when she says, "I've created a nine-to-five job for myself, but it's satisfying because it's mine." She tries to keep office hours between 10:00 A.M. and 3:00 P.M., but that rarely works. "I do the work until the job is done."

It's work she clearly enjoys. "I like conceiving of albums, of producing them, of dreaming up the artwork. I like marketing, and I like selling the albums." Then she adds, "I like trying to get reviewed." A fat binder of clippings from magazines and newspapers is proof of her success.

Maggie spends less

time in the office when she is working on her own music, whether practicing or recording. "Things slow down when I'm not here," she says. But it's unavoidable, particularly during the summer when she performs a lot, both as a soloist and with groups.

If running Maggie's Music and performing sounds like too much for one person, it is. A part-time secretary and a once-a-week bookkeeper keep Maggie's business running smoothly.

Instead of producing the albums that are sold under her record label, she now hires a

Maggie works at her desk at Maggie's Music.

producer. She has also decided not to do much touring. "I'm kind of a homebody," she says. It wasn't always this way.

Street Music and More

Maggie grew up in Florida, the daughter of an advertising copywriter mother and a cartoonist father who played jazz piano. "He was my inspiration," she says. She started piano lessons at eight, adding classical guitar and bassoon during her junior year of high school. A bassoon scholarship took her to the summer Eastern Music Festival in North Carolina.

Maggie had no intention of studying music. Instead, she studied art. But music didn't leave her life. She has both a natural talent for sight-reading and for finding musicians to play with. "I just never planned to make money with music," she says. She says she never expected that Maggie's Music would sell more than half a million records in its first few years.

After graduating from college, Maggie crisscrossed the country from Maryland to California, then back to Maryland. She learned survival skills, taking part-time secretarial jobs to cover her living expenses. She also found outlets for her musical interests and enormous energy: from street music gigs to teaching private lessons on many instruments. In Maryland she volunteered to organize a concert series through a local arts organization, which helped her "find out about the local music scene."

When a musician performs a piece of music for the first time without studying or practicing it beforehand, he or she is *sight-reading.*

"Somehow," Maggie says, "I was always able to sell myself. So I thought nothing of advertising or of going into cafes or museum shops and telling them I would play." She has found some unusual gigs over the years, including Maryland's Renaissance Festival, an annual fair recreating the entertainment, food, and characters found in Renaissance England. "It has been great training," she says. "I learned how to attract people to my music."

A Jack of All Trades

Since self-promotion is a skill that doesn't come easily to most musicians, Maggie had an advantage when she formed her own

> ❝ **You must believe in what you are doing. If you are enthusiastic and honest, it comes through.** ❞

record company. She credits her art background with helping her develop quality album or CD covers and advertising campaigns. She also writes the album notes and ads and handles the financial side of Maggie's Music. Like most small business owners, and unlike most large record company executives, she performs many of the day-to-day tasks in addition to managing

Maggie Sansone

the company. To stay current with the recording industry, she reads books about the music business and takes courses on entertainment law and recording techniques.

Maggie also believes you can't be shy. "It's important to be charming, personable, talented, pleasant, and to be able to talk about what you love to do in a way that excites other people," she says. "You must believe in what you are doing. If you are enthusiastic and honest, it comes through."

But owning a record company is also stressful. "You have to be constantly on your toes," she says. "And you must deal with rejection. You need to be prepared mentally and keep a positive attitude."

Musicians perform at a renaissance festival.

The Music of the People

The future is bright, she thinks, for her company and for folk music. Maggie's Music is already a financial success, with critically acclaimed albums and good sales. Maggie's goal is to find enough time to expand her business and still perform. She nods at the Scottish small pipe, still in its case on the shelf, waiting to be played. "This is the music of the people. It will endure. The more technical our society becomes, the more people crave traditions and roots and culture." After all, she says, "'Greensleeves' is probably three hundred years old and people are still performing it."

As for the future of the music recording business, she thinks for a minute. "There's a lot of competition out there," she says. "Find a niche, a specialty. And pursue what you love. You have to take the risk of being poor," she adds, "but not in a dreary way."

"Knowledge is important," Maggie says. "You can get it at school or by yourself. It's also a good idea to get involved in your local music community, maybe by volunteering at the arts council." She has a final thought: "You could look for part-time jobs in your field and develop yourself that way. Whatever you do," she says, "you can't operate in a vacuum." Playing or singing with other musicians is essential to any musician's development and growth.

DANCE UPON THE SHORE

MAGGIE SANSONE

A reel Celtic voyage with traditional tunes and innovative new sounds from Ireland, Scotland and Brittany featuring hammered dulcimer

Joel Lewis

Chapter Ten

VOCALIST

"nce I hear something, I can sing it," says singer Joel Lewis. It doesn't matter if it's been 10 minutes or 10 years, the tune stays with him. And since his voice ranges from high to low, he can sing either tenor or bass. Both musical gifts have served him well during his 18-year music career in the U.S. Navy.

For the last 11 years, Joel has been lead vocalist with the Electric Brigade, a nine-member unit of the U.S. Naval Academy band. In addition to Joel, there is another singer, a trumpeter, a saxophonist, a keyboardist, a drummer, a percussionist, a guitar player, and a bass player. The ninth member is the soundman.

The Electric Brigade is usually described as a Top 40 band, a description Joel thinks is inaccurate. Whose top 40? he wants to know. "We play songs by Prince and the Four Tops and the Beach Boys and Nat King Cole." His greatest joy has always been pleasing the audience. "Even when I am doing music I don't like, I like to look into the audience. If they are happy, it's satisfying."

Singing in the Military

Singing with the Electric Brigade means Joel has an irregular schedule—working weekends and evenings and touring for up to eight weeks each year. The group plays mostly for schools and community groups. Although a navy operations office schedules concerts three months in advance, "open days" are filled on shorter notice. Since rehearsals are scheduled around performances and tours, Joel's hours can vary widely.

When he is not on tour, performing, or rehearsing, Joel reads *Billboard* magazine to see what tunes are popular. He also scouts music stores, listens to CDs, and talks to people to find out what music they are listening to. Before choosing songs, he also listens carefully to the lyrics to make sure they are suitable for young children. And to keep his voice in shape, he practices every day.

> # You always have to respect somebody else's musical ideas.

Once a year, the band takes a break from concerts and works on new programs for two weeks. "It's intense," says Joel. "We read through the music, learn the vocals, then sit down and put the vocals with the playing. Then it goes to memorization." And there is the choreography—or dance routine—to learn. MTV, he says, has made that important.

Natural Talent

Joel grew up in Atlanta—and later California—listening to his grandmother sing in the church choir. As part of a group named "The Choraleers," he made an album and toured Europe when he was 14. Joel began doing backup vocals for recording studios when a producer for a record company heard him sing. Because he could not read music, he got by on natural talent. A tune would be played, and he would sing what he heard. Reading music, he says today, is a much more efficient way to learn a song. "Singers were getting a bad rap," he says. "They were taking too much time to learn things because they hadn't had any music training."

After high school, Joel entered college to study commercial art. "I always loved to draw," he says. But art wasn't for him, and he dropped out and joined the navy. After basic training, an officer saw his resume and suggested he take a music audition. He passed and was sent to the School of Music in Norfolk, Virginia. "Getting in," he says, "is no guarantee. You can fail this school."

But Joel was in his element. Within six months, he had learned to read and arrange music and to play the piano. There were courses in harmony and ear training. After graduating seventh in his class, he auditioned to be a vocalist with one of the navy's bands. He was assigned to a navy band in San Diego, a job he kept for five years.

Learning to recognize and write down musical pitches, intervals, and rhythms is called *ear training.*

Joel Lewis

When he is not on tour, Joel has more time to practice his music.

In the meantime, Joel had received offers from several record companies. His band director told him, "Try it. If it doesn't work, we'll take you back." So Joel left, only to find that recording companies were no longer offering steady salaries with their contracts. He soon rejoined the navy, this time as the vocalist assigned to a band in Rhode Island.

After several busy years, he auditioned for the Electric Brigade in Annapolis, Maryland.

"At that time it was a country-and-western band," he says. "The navy wanted a popular music band instead." Today Joel is assistant director of the Electric Brigade, a job that carries programming responsibilities in addition to performing. He also does solo guest appearances with the U.S. Naval Academy's concert band.

Dealing with the Stress

Singing in the Electric Brigade is not without stress.

"You have to sing songs by different writers and in different styles," he says. Then there's the heavy lifting. "We are our own roadies," he says, describing how band members lug their own equipment. He also mentions that the group sometimes encounters indifferent audiences. But most difficult for Joel to handle is the burnout that he and the other musicians face during weeks of exhausting schedules and heavy travel. "It happens if we are fatigued," he says.

Music in the Military

The army, the navy, the marines, and the air force all have music programs. There is a U.S. military band in every state except Nevada, and bands are stationed in Europe, Asia, and Latin America.

To qualify, you must first pass the Armed Services Vocational Aptitude Battery Test and go through basic training. Assignments are made on the basis of auditions and openings. The competition is fierce, particularly for the "special" bands. These include the service academy bands and the highly visible bands in Washington that play for government occasions. In some cases and in some branches, musicians perform other duties as well.

A Singing Career

Only a few lucky *singers* ever become rich and famous. Tony Bennett, Whitney Houston, and Garth Brooks are the exceptions, not the rule. But many unknowns have singing careers. Some have solo careers, but most work as part of a group. The work is usually part time, and the pay varies. There are no formal education requirements, but most professional singers read music and are good at sight-reading— singing a piece of music through for the first time.

Professional singers work in clubs, music theaters, rock or country bands, jazz ensembles, choral societies, opera companies, and synagogue and church choirs. *Backup* or *studio singers* do commercial recordings, movie sound tracks, and radio and television commercials. A studio singer needs talent, skill at sight-reading, flexibility, persistence, business sense, and an ability to sing different styles. Backup singers also need a great demo tape and word-of-mouth referrals. Most live near large cities, especially New York and Los Angeles.

Joel thinks versatility, an ability to work with others, and hard work have helped make him become successful. "You have to practice. You have to want to get better." He suggests that someone who wants a music career in the military should "absorb everything you can about music, read about it, listen to jazz, to rhythm and blues, to everything. Understand it." He underlines the importance of learning to accept criticism and to "being open-minded toward different kinds of music. You always have to respect somebody else's musical ideas." Besides, he says, "music is on and off the job. You can get together with other musicians after hours."

When asked about musical careers in the military within the next century, Joel laughs and says, "Bands will be gone when the military is gone." The military, he knows, will always need bands for both public relations and ceremonial duties.

As for his own career, Joel plans another twist. After retiring from the navy in two years, he will return to school to prepare for a second, different career. "I want to make music my hobby again. I want to write music," he says. "It's not so important for me to perform anymore."

Seth Knopp

Chapter Eleven

CLASSICAL PIANIST

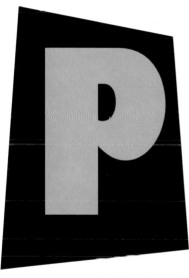

eople take music for granted," says classical pianist Seth Knopp. "Music is the first language. It begins with our first heartbeat. It touches us at a basic level. Music makes people cry and laugh." And music's language, Seth believes, is a way for people to communicate with each other. "If music were taught at an early age, it could bring people together. I don't see how people can cut music programs in schools."

Seth and his wife, French-Canadian violinist Violaine Melançon, are two-thirds of the Peabody Trio, which includes cellist Thomas Kraines. In 1989 the trio won the celebrated Naumburg Award for chamber music. The victory put their career in high gear. "Competitions give you a stamp of approval," Seth says. "People suddenly take you more seriously, but you know you are the same person you were the day before. Winning may get you a concert or a spurt of concerts, but even winners are not assured of a career."

Performing

Seth's workday runs "from 10:30 A.M. to 3:30 P.M., six days a week." The trio rehearses together most days. Seth also teaches at Peabody Conservatory. "Sometimes we go three or four weeks without a day off," he says. There are concerts and numerous tours. And each summer they spend five weeks teaching at the Waldon School for young composers in New Hampshire.

"Music is not nine-to-five. You don't leave it in the office," Seth says. "I can't imagine life without music. Music is a deep way of expressing ideas. Performing is special. You are the link between the composer and the listener. It's a sort of holy mission."

A Career

A career. It's a magic word in the world of classical music, one that means concert bookings in places like New York and San Francisco, summer music festivals, international concert tours, and the opportunity to teach at world-class schools. By these standards, Seth is well into a career.

Seth's career was launched when he was six, the year he began taking private piano lessons. He remembers a house full of music as his parents listened to classical recordings and the songs of Cole Porter, Billie Holliday, and folk singer Pete Seeger. As for the piano, "I loved to play right away." So much so, he says, "that the neighbors complained when I started to practice too early in the morning."

Family moves, from Wisconsin to Chicago

Conducting

Chamber groups play without a *conductor,* but orchestras, bands, and larger ensembles cannot. Conductors lead a group of musicians through a piece of music—directing the tempo, pointing out entrances and changes in dynamics, and making sure the different sounds are blended into a unified whole. Conducting is a very visible career in which only a few musicians become world famous. It is, however, an overcrowded field in which there are few full-time jobs. Many young conductors get their start doing part-time con- ducting for com- munity or school orchestras, audi- tioning for better jobs as they gain experience. Con- ducting styles vary from reserved to flamboyant. What is most important for a conductor is a pro-

found understanding of many types of serious music and a forceful view of how that music should be inter- preted. Instrumental conducting is a major in most col- lege music programs, but most conductors also play an instrument such as violin or piano. Other conduc- tors specialize in choral conducting. Many also have solo performance careers. Some also compose.

Seth Knopp

to Philadelphia, sent Seth to a series of schools. "I had only a few friends interested in music," he says. And although he played for some high school musicals, there weren't many opportunities for a pianist. Pianos aren't regularly called for in band or orchestra music, although they are needed to accompany soloists. But Seth continued to take private lessons from a series of "wonderful teachers." And he practiced, as much as five hours a day from the time he was 11 or 12.

Following his college years at Boston's New England Conservatory, Seth met Violaine Melançon. They quickly formed both a personal and professional partnership. They both enrolled in the San Francisco Conservatory. To earn money and gain experience, he says,

In addition to rehearsing with the trio, Seth practices alone.

"I was gigging, and Violaine was gigging," and they both taught private lessons. More importantly, they began to play duos and trios.

Seth and Violaine auditioned for the United States Information Agency's Artistic Ambassador Program. The duo soon found themselves touring Europe, Asia, and the

Middle East for seven weeks, bringing American music to other parts of the world. It was their first big tour, one that Seth remembers as fun but much too long.

During this time, Seth was studying privately with renowned pianist Leon Fleisher at Peabody Conservatory in Baltimore. Seth, Violaine, and a cellist formed a trio. Peabody Conservatory soon hired them as an "Ensemble in Residence," to be called the Peabody Trio. They played concerts and coached student ensembles. Both Seth and Violaine are now full-time faculty members.

Chamber Music

"Chamber music," says Seth, "is a wonderful thing and a difficult thing. The life of a chamber musician is learning how to work with other people. Some groups get along fine and others don't talk to each other."

He also believes that a classical chamber musician can be either outgoing or shy and private. "The number one priority," Seth says, "is to love the music."

He also believes musicians change and develop. "You go through stages of development. It's very important to perform and to find a teacher who is wonderful."

How?

"Take a few lessons, get a feel for how the person teaches and what their ideals are."

Practicing the piano or any instrument seriously requires many long, solitary hours. Seth also encourages playing with others and making friends with other musicians. Because the piano is largely a solo instrument, he feels he missed out on some of the musical friendships that exist among band, orchestra, and choir members during their school years. "It's important," he says, "to have people with whom to share ideas about music.

And what about natural talent? "Talent is important, but a lot of people are talented," Seth says. "You won't know how talented you are until you start playing." He warns against discouragement. "There are ideals to strive for at every stage," he says.

An Artistic Pursuit

Like many musicians, Seth has had to deal with stage fright. "It comes about when you want to be perfect," he says. Early in his career, stage fright made him "hysterical with nerves." But experience has given him insight. "An artistic pursuit is about the pursuit. It's not about arriving anywhere. The important thing is to learn and develop." And although he still gets nervous before a concert, it's not so bad anymore. "I have a normal life. I can eat the day of the concert."

Handling rejection is another big problem for some musicians. "I think musicians tend to ignore good reviews and remember only the bad ones," he says. He points out that being an artist means trial and error. "With musicians, their trials are public and their errors are public." Seth insists that a musician can't be successful all the time. After all, he says, a review is only the opinion of one person.

The Future

Seth is optimistic about his future. He believes the Peabody Trio will have the chance to commission music, hiring composers to write new pieces for them. He expects the trio will also make recordings and promote chamber music and music education at Peabody Conservatory and through summer programs. Although he looks forward to it all, he's willing to let his career unfold at its own pace.

But when asked about the future of serious chamber music itself—with its dwindling public and private funds and small audiences—Seth grows quiet. "We are going

> **Music is not nine-to-five. You don't leave it in the office.**

through hard times right now," he says. "But things can change." He calls on kids and their parents to demand more music in their schools. "Together they could make things happen. There would be more music."

Henry Wong

Chapter Twelve

Music Retailer

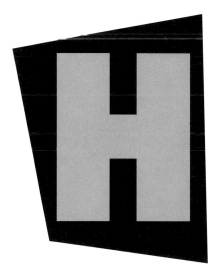

enry Wong, owner of two CD stores, is wearing a T-shirt that says "I Love Opera." It's a clue to his curious career path: from scientist to thriving music entrepreneur, or businessperson.

Trained as a biochemist, Henry did medical research for seven years after college. On long Saturday afternoons, as he did experiments in his laboratory, he began to listen to the Metropolitan Opera's broadcasts from New York. Soon he was going to the opera and reading books on music. "I always enjoyed instrumental music," he says. "Then I discovered the beauty of opera."

Other People's Money

Henry is a typical small businessman who does many jobs that an executive at a large CD retailer would delegate to others. He also works long hours without complaint, often 12 or 14 hours at a stretch. "If you employ other people or take other people's money, you are morally responsible. You go home when the job is done."

As the owner of the company, he spends much of each day on the phone. He also plans the advertising and marketing and does some of the purchasing. But the majority of Henry's day is spent handling the finances for his business. "You need to control the profit and loss of the company," he says. Without previous business experience, he admits to some early mistakes. But he says he learned from them. "You have got to know a bit of everything," he says. "The key is to be well-rounded. You have to know every area."

The Music Nuts

For most people, enjoying music is enough. But for Henry, music was to play a larger role. He blames six friends, "the music nuts," who later became his business partners. When they talked about opening a record store, he listened. Then he got involved.

Still employed as a full-time researcher, Henry worked part time at a record store to learn the business firsthand. He also wrote a business plan and did his market research. Some of it was as simple as visiting record stores, studying the CDs they sold, counting how many clerks were at work and how many customers were in the store. "Basic common sense," he calls it.

His store, *An Die Musik*—which means "to music" in German—was two years in the planning stages. That was six years ago. Now he owns two stores. He sells "not just classical and jazz, but also pop, rock, rap,

" I wish I could predict where the retail music industry is headed. "

everything." And he has only minor nostalgia for the science career he left behind.

A Willingness to Learn

Henry did not grow up in a family of musicians. He does not play an instrument. He has no business background. So he was forced to rely on his willingness to learn and, most of all, his unshakable belief in hard work.

"Being smart helps," he says, "but dedication helps more. And you need to deal with people. And make friends," he adds.

After opening An Die Musik, Henry took his own advice, forming friendships with the DJs at local radio stations. He invited musicians, such as Baltimore Symphony conductor David Zinman, to do album

Retail Music Careers

Many of Henry's employees are musicians or music students. He hires them to work behind the scenes and out front with customers. *Sales clerks, buyers,* and *managers* are promoted from within as they learn the business. His buyers often specialize in a certain kind of music, as do his clerks. Many clerks work part time, which can make scheduling difficult.

Employees in large retail chain stores may not know the owner, but their jobs are similar. A background in music is useful, although not required. Most store employees learn the business on the job. Other retail careers can be found in stores that sell musical instruments and sheet music. A formal music background is often vital, particularly if a store sells to professional musicians.

Sheet music publishing is a retail subspecialty. Music publishers can be large or small. A background in music is practical, although most jobs require a combination of business and publishing skills, such as editing and copywriting, finance and law, sales and marketing, and graphics and printing.

signings or to perform. These guests drew crowds to the store.

Some of Henry's other schemes made his large chain store competitors laugh at him, he remembers. When his first store opened in 1991, all CDs were sold in long plastic containers. The waste bothered him, so he had his staff repackage each CD and recycle the plastic.

Henry also let his customers listen to albums before they bought, a practice that was then unheard of. But Henry has had the last laugh. Not only did he find loyal customers, CDs are now packaged in half the plastic they once were.

Henry's own satisfaction comes from working with customers and staff. "If customers come to the store, they have made a special effort," he says. "We offer coffee. We strike up conversations. We let you listen to CDs. People come to socialize." And most important, people come back.

The Human Factor

The most difficult parts of Henry's job? "I wish I could predict where the retail music industry is headed," he says with a sigh. And then there's what Henry calls the "human factor." With 50 floor clerks, buyers, and managers—many of them part-timers who are also musicians—he has to manage different styles and work habits. "You have to maximize their talents. And there is," he says, "a big difference between what you want to get done and what actually gets done."

Henry Wong

He believes it's his responsibility to be a good boss. "Your staff has to have confidence in you."

"Every Day You Learn"

It is very important for Henry to know his industry, the community, and what's happening in the world. He reads newspapers and magazines and tries to stay on top of the technology. The future of his business depends on it. For now,

Henry discusses newly released CDs with one of his clerks.

he has decided not to open more stores, preferring to give his current two a chance to grow. "Every day you learn. You have to change and be flexible."

He also mentions the uncertainty of the retail music business in the future. "Machines may make CDs, delivering them through fiber optics, through computers. Anything can happen. It will be determined by the record manufacturers and by the technology. In the future, CDs could be sold through home shopping networks." If that happens, he says, "I will work out of the basement of my house."

And if you have a great idea for a music business? "It's important to write a business plan," says Henry, "and do a reality check with someone else." He also believes that a solid education in business is a good idea. "You have to be concrete about the bottom line. You have to know the business, do the fundamentals, and get feedback. I took a calculated risk," he says. "But you need a degree of sureness. And you need room to retreat if it doesn't work."

TO CONTINUE EXPLORING...

American Association for Music Therapy
P.O. Box 80012
Valley Forge, PA 19484
(610) 265-4006

American Choral Directors Association
   (ACDA)
P.O. Box 6310
Lawton, OK 73506
(405) 355-8161

American Federation of Violin and Bow
   Makers (AFVBM)
167 Cabrillo Street
Costa Mesa, CA 92627
(800) 633-2777

American Guild of Organists (AGO)
475 Riverside Drive, Suite 1260
New York, NY 10115
(212) 870-2310

American Musical Instrument Society (AMIS)
c/o Albert R. Rice
1664 Corbin Avenue
Tarzana, CA 91356-1011
(818) 776-9446

American Music Center (AMC)
(for composers, performers, students, and
   other music professionals)
30 W. 26th Street, Suite 1001
New York, NY 10010-2011
(212) 366-5260

American Society of Composers, Authors, and
   Publishers
1 Lincoln Plaza
New York, NY 10023
(212) 595-3050

American Symphony Orchestra League
777 14th Street N.W., Suite 500
Washington, DC 20005
(202) 628-0099

Association of Arts Administration Educators
   (AAAE)
c/o J. Dennis Rich
Columbia College Chicago
600 S. Michigan Avenue
Chicago, IL 60605
(312) 663-1600

The Blues Foundation (TBF)
   (for musicians, writers, music promoters,
   record producers, and blues fans)
174 Beale Street
Memphis, TN 38103
(901) 527-BLUE

Chorus America
1811 Chestnut Street, Suite 401
Philadelphia, PA 19103
(215) 563-2430

Classical Music Broadcasters Association
   (CMBA)
c/o KKHI
1600 Smith Street, Suite 5100
Houston, TX 77002
(415) 986-2151

Contemporary A Cappella Society of America
   (CASA)
1850 Union Street, Suite 1441
San Francisco, CA 94123
(415) 563-5224

Gospel Music Workshop of America (GMWA)
3908 W. Warren Street
Detroit, MI 48208
(313) 898-2340

Independent Music Association (IMA)
   (helps promote, market, and distribute
   independently produced music)
c/o Don Kulak
317 Skyline Lake Drive
Ringwood, NJ 07456
(201) 831-1317

International Federation of Children's Choirs
   (FICE)
Shallway Building
120 S. 3rd Street
Connellsville, PA 15425
(412) 628-8000

International Society of Performing Arts
   Administrators (ISPAA)
2920 Fuller Avenue N.E., Suite 205
Grand Rapids, MI 49505-3458
(616) 364-3000

Metropolitan Opera Guild
70 Lincoln Center Plaza, 6th floor
New York, NY 10023
(212) 769-7000

Music Educators National Conference
(MENC)
1806 Robert Fulton Drive
Reston, VA 22091
(703) 860-4000

Music Publishers' Association of the United
States (MPA)
c/o NMPA/HFA
711 3rd Avenue
New York, NY 10018

Music Teachers National Association
441 Vine Street, Suite 505
Cincinnati, OH 45202
(513) 421-1420

National Academy of Recording Arts &
Sciences
3402 Pico Boulevard
Santa Monica, CA 90405
(310) 392-3777

National Academy of Songwriters (NAS)
6381 Hollywood Boulevard, Suite 780
Hollywood, CA 90028
(213) 463-7178

National Association for Music Therapy
8455 Colesville Road, Suite 930
Silver Spring, MD 20910
(301) 589-3300

National Association of Accompanists and
Coaches (NAAC)
(covers chamber music, opera coaching,
and accompaniment of the piano)
395 Riverside Drive, Suite 13A
New York, NY 10025
(212) 316-6164

National Association of Broadcast Employees
and Technicians
501 3rd Street N.W., 8th floor
Washington, DC 20001
(202) 434-1254

National Association of Music Merchants
(NAMM)
5140 Avenida Encinas
Carlsbad, CA 92008
(619) 438-8001

National Association of Recording
Merchandisers (NARM)
9 Eves Drive, Suite 120
Marlton, NJ 08053
(609) 596-2221

National Public Radio (NPR)
635 Massachusetts Avenue N.W.
Washington, DC 20001
(202) 414-2000

Percussive Arts Society (PAS)
P.O. Box 25
Lawton, OK 73502
(405) 353-1455

Recording Industry Association of America
1020 19th Street N.W., Suite 200
Washington, DC 20036
(202) 775-0101

Society of Professional Audio Recording
Services (SPARS)
4300 10th Avenue N.
Lake Worth, FL 33461
(407) 641-6648

Songwriters Guild of America
1500 Harbor Boulevard
Weehawken, NJ 07087-6732
(201) 867-7603

U.S. Air Force Bands and Music Programs
SAF/PAC
1690 Air Force Pentagon
Washington, DC 20330-1690
(703) 695-0019

U.S. Marine Band "President's Own"
(oldest professional band in the U.S.)
8th and I Streets S.E.
Washington, DC 20390-5000
(202) 433-5810

U.S. Navy
Special Assistant for Music
(PERS-6MM)
Chief of Naval Personnel
Washington, DC 20370-6000
(703) 693-0513

Violin Society of America (VSA)
85-07 Abingdon Road
Kew Gardens, NY 11415
(718) 849-1373

INDEX

ABOUT THE AUTHOR

Barbara Lee is the author of *Death in Still Waters: A Chesapeake Bay Mystery,* which won St. Martin's Press' 1994 Best First Malice Domestic Mystery Novel Contest. A New Yorker, she now lives in Maryland.

ACKNOWLEDGMENTS

The photographs have been reproduced through the courtesy of: Andy King, pp. 2, 6, 10, 12, 15, 17, 20, 24, 25, 26, 28, 31, 32, 35, 36, 39, 40, 44, 47, 48, 52, 54, 55, 59, 60, 63, 66, 68, 73, 74, 76, 79, 81, 84, 86, 88, 92, 96, 98, 100, 103, 106; Visuals Unlimited/© Mark Skalny, p. 8; Visuals Unlimited/Emily Stong, p. 18; Nancy Smedstad/IPS, p. 22; Minnesota Orchestra, p. 23; Charlie Byrd Trio poster, p. 33; © Carol Pratt, pp. 41, 42; Washington National Cathedral/Ken Cobb, pp. 46, 51, 95; Visuals Unlimited/ Mark E. Gibson, p. 49; © Steven Ferry, p. 56; © Shmuel Thaler, pp. 65, 90; © Frances M. Roberts, p. 71; © Jim West, p. 82; Maggie Sansone, p. 83; © Richard B. Levine, p. 89; IPS, p. 104.

Front and back cover photographs by Andy King.